Joggers

A Play

Geraldine Aron

A Samuel French Acting Edition

SAMUEL FRENCH

FOUNDED 1830

SAMUELFRENCH-LONDON.CO.UK
SAMUELFRENCH.COM

JOGGERS is fully protected under the copyright laws of the British Commonwealth, including Canada, the United States of America, and all other countries of the Copyright Union. All rights, including professional and amateur stage productions, recitation, lecturing, public reading, motion picture, radio broadcasting, television and the rights of translation into foreign languages are strictly reserved.

ISBN 978-0-573-12124-1

www.samuelfrench-london.co.uk

www.samuelfrench.com

FOR AMATEUR PRODUCTION ENQUIRIES

UNITED KINGDOM AND WORLD EXCLUDING NORTH AMERICA
plays@SamuelFrench-London.co.uk
020 7255 4302/01

Each title is subject to availability from Samuel French,

depending upon country of performance.

CAUTION: Professional and amateur producers are hereby warned that *JOGGERS* is subject to a licensing fee. Publication of this play does not imply availability for performance. Both amateurs and professionals considering a production are strongly advised to apply to the appropriate agent before starting rehearsals, advertising, or booking a theatre. A licensing fee must be paid whether the title is presented for charity or gain and whether or not admission is charged.

The professional rights in this play are controlled by Samuel French Ltd, 52 Fitzroy Street, London, W1T 5JR.

CHARACTERS

Walter Shapiro (Wally)
Augustus Armstrong (Gus)
Norma Shapiro
Sylvie Armstrong

The action takes place on the beach and on the lawns of
a hotel in a seaside resort, during the course of one week

Time—the present

<table>
<tr><td>Scene 1</td><td>The beach</td></tr>
<tr><td>Scene 2</td><td>The hotel lawns</td></tr>
<tr><td>Scene 3</td><td>The beach</td></tr>
<tr><td>Scene 4</td><td>The hotel lawns</td></tr>
<tr><td>Scene 5</td><td>The beach</td></tr>
</table>

Joggers was first performed at Brian Astbury's Space Theatre in
Cape Town, South Africa in 1979. Derek Lyndon, Ken Berry,
Sue Hanson and Yvonne Copley were directed by Roland
Stafford, who also designed the sets.

For Richard

PRODUCTION NOTES

When *Joggers* was first staged, a small budget inspired the following simple but very effective sets:

The beach was indicated by a couple of polystyrene rocks on which the characters sat from time to time. A few pebbles were scattered around, and there was also a small mound of sand for sifting purposes. The main prop was an umbrella holder in which a sign with a SWIMMING symbol was stood. The scene change from the beach to the hotel lawns was done by two scene shifters dressed as hotel waiters who removed the rocks etc. and wheeled on two beach loungers and a small table. The SWIMMING sign was replaced by a beach umbrella, which was then opened. Norma and Sylvie walked on during this and thanked the waiters for their trouble. The background remained the same for all scenes—it was a sort of cellophane curtain with a fluffy cloud pinned to it.

The luxury hotel aspect was covered by borrowing thick towels from an authentic hotel chain, and by silly drinks, abrim with flowers and fruit, served in coconut or pineapple shells.

Music to cover the scene changes should be chosen with great care so that it has relevance to the play. In the original production, contemporary music from the Top Twenty was used, with or without lyrics, but selected for its mood—the play opened with something cheerful for jogging, Sylvie's weeping was accompanied by a nostalgic piece, and so on.

JOGGERS

SCENE 1

The beach. Early morning

There are a couple of rocks (polystyrene) big enough to sit on, some pebbles and a small mound of sand for sifting. A SWIMMING sign stands in an umbrella holder. Off stage L is the hotel and off stage R is a continuing stretch of beach. The audience is the sea

When the Lights come up, Wally is jogging earnestly. A successful and prosperous businessman, he has recently become interested in fitness. He is wearing a tracksuit, and is clearly a man of good taste, well-groomed. His jogging style is short—knees low, chin up. His nostrils flare with effort. There is a Black-out, during which Wally removes his tracksuit. As the Lights come up again, Wally is towelling himself dry, as if he has just come out of the water. He bellows and springs about, scrubs at his chest-hair, tosses his head, puffs out his cheeks, bares his teeth, jiggles his jowls, etc.

Gus enters R and stands slightly up stage, watching Wally. Gus is also in his mid-forties, but he is smaller and less prosperous than Wally. He has dreadful taste in swimwear, and wears a comb in the waistband of his leopard-skin scants. At the moment he is wearing a vest and shorts over his trunks, and is carrying a hotel towel. Gus has also been jogging. In fact, he has been following Wally and is now looking forward to making his acquaintance. Slightly breathless, he watches Wally, a friendly smile ready, then nods cheerfully

Gus How's the water this morning?

Wally (*noticing him for the first time*) Champagne!

Gus You can't beat it, eh—specially after a spot of exercise.

Wally Sets you up for the day—a real tonic. You been in yet?

Gus Not yet. To tell you the truth, I'm more of a pool man myself.

Wally You're kidding! You mean you'd rather swim in that mixture of chemicals and urine than in this? Well, each to his own. (*He sits on one of the rocks and takes from beneath it a plastic bag containing a bottle of petrol and a wad of cotton-wool. He begins to remove scabs of oil from the soles of his feet*)

Gus That's a good idea, keeping a supply of that handy. I was just saying to my wife yesterday, the hotel should keep a kit like that in the lobby. I said to her, I said "It's no use them complaining about oil on the carpeting if they're not interested in supplying the means to get it off." It's obvious really, don't you think?

Wally Did you mention it to the manager?

Gus (*after a pause*) No, I didn't, but I intend to. They ask you for your comments when you leave. I told the wife I might put it on the card, as a suggestion. Better late than never, eh?

Wally Oh, are you at the end of your stay then?

Gus No fear—we only arrived yesterday. Another six days to go. And you?

Wally We've booked in for three weeks. (*He consults his watch*) One down and two to go. (*He slaps his belly*) I've never felt better.

Gus Three weeks, eh? I didn't know you could come for three weeks. We had a choice between the fifteen-day Bonanza or the seven-day Getaway Plan. Being as it's our first time here we went for the Getaway. Didn't want to risk our entire leave, you know how it is. (*He shakes his head, remembering*) Whew. Wouldn't be the first time. So what do they call your package?

Wally We're not on a package.

Gus Oh. Then it must be costing you a bomb. My wife and I worked it out last night; all meals would stand you in for almost *twice* the cost of an inclusive package. Now me and Sylvie can eat ourselves silly three times a day and it doesn't cost us a bean. Personally, I've never been able to see why anyone would be stupid enough to go it alone when they could be enjoying a package. Work it out for yourself: they flew us here, collected us from the airport in a luxury coach. We get full board, plus two half-day tours to the Cango Caves and the Wilderness, a welcoming cocktail party with free drinks, the lot! And all for less than the price of a week at ordinary bed and breakfast rates.

Wally I don't know how they do it and make a profit.

Gus Because of suckers like you—that's how they do it! (*He stops*) No offence meant—but it does make you think, you must admit.

Wally My wife and I prefer to be independent. She doesn't like package tours.

Gus But what's not to like? We all sleep in the same rooms, all get the same grub, don't we? Just give me one example of how it's an advantage to be freelance, as it were.

Wally Mmmm, let's see. Well, for one thing, the freelancers don't have to wear armbands with "Cheapskate" written on them.

Gus (*after a pause*) That's a good one! Armbands with—wait till I tell Sylvie that. She'll have a good laugh!

Wally Then again, we're not sprayed with D.D.T. as we come through the doors, we can have as many baths as we like and if we don't want to have singsongs in the bar we get a special dispensation.

Gus (*laughing*) A special dis—I can see you've got a good sense of humour, anyway. And that's more important than a head for business, eh. D.D.T.! My name's Gus, Gus Armstrong, Jo'burg.

Wally Wally Shapiro, Cape Town.

They shake hands. Gus cleans his feet with the petrol, sitting on the other rock. Wally stands up and does some breathing exercises

I knew a Rhodesian called Angus. Red-haired bloke. Used to farm tobacco up there. Got out just in time by the looks of it. Converted his cash into Persian carpets and set up a wholesale business in Aberdeen.

Gus That so? Nice crowd, the Scots. Although actually—just to put the record straight—I'm not actually an Angus. I'm more of an Augustus, if the truth be known. Not a name I particularly like, but what can you do.

Wally Oh, I see.

Gus I've known the odd Shapiro, though. My dentist is a Shapiro. The wife won't go to him because he hasn't got this new laughing-gas business. But I reckon a bit of pain never killed anyone, so I'm not changing. Then there was Shapiro Agnew . . .

Wally Spiro.

Gus I beg yours?

Wally Spiro Agnew. A Greek.

Gus (*after a pause*) You know, I believe you're right. Well, let's see, that little ballerina, Phyllis Shapiro. Wonderful! Terrific! Saw her on the telly.

Wally Spira.

Gus (*after a pause*) Ah well, what's in a name, as Shakespeare said. Don't know about you, but I reckon I'm just about ready to tuck into the old bacon and eggs. Are you a breakfast man, Wally?

Wally Coffee and toast, usually.

Gus That wouldn't do for us, not on holiday. Mind you, I can understand it—the prices they charge if you're not on a package!

Both men stand. Wally conceals his bottle of petrol, etc. beneath the rock and drapes his towel around his shoulders. Suddenly he and Gus adopt more controlled stances. They pull in their tummies, looking off L

Lovely looking girl that. I saw her on the dance floor last night. I said to my wife—I'll bet that one's a handful the way she's carrying on. Everything hanging out, the hair flying around. Had a drop too much, I'd say. Still, it's different on holiday really . . . She must be searching for pansy shells . . . People get away with murder on holiday. Take on another identity in a way. All part of the fun. Sylvie and I spend hours guessing what people do before we meet them. You ever played the guessing game, Wally?

Wally You mean wondering if people are having dirty week-ends, that sort of thing?

Gus Oh, not necessarily that. More if they're well-off or not. Where they're from. Package tour or freelance, ha ha. (*He slaps Wally's back*) Take our shapely young beachcomber, Sylvie's christened her the Sex Bomb. Say we're sitting in the bar, enjoying a cocktail . . . Suddenly Sylvie will say to me, casual-like, "Don't look now, but here comes S.B!" Then there's T.W. —that's Tight Wad, and C.H.—that's—well, and so on.

Wally C.H.?

Gus Ach, it's just a silly game we play amongst ourselves. Harmless. Between ourselves.

Wally Sure. So what's C.H.?

Gus Chopped Herring. Nothing ethnic or anything. Just our little joke.

Wally Chopped Herring. Chopped Herring—that'll be the woman in the white dress, with the turban. Am I right?

Gus Ach, I wish now I'd never mentioned it.

Wally Am I right though?

Gus Now, look Wally, it's only a little joke. Nothing malicious. If it's your wife, I wouldn't want you . . .

Wally (*laughing*) Relax, relax. You're in the clear.

Gus (*relieved*) Whew. Wait till I tell Sylvie this lot. B.M. she calls me when I put my foot in it—meaning Big Mouth! What's your time, Wal?

Wally (*looking at his watch*) Ten to eight.

Gus Well, I think I'll wend my way. I've made a plan to jog every morning, so perhaps we'll meet again.

Wally Right. And enjoy your stay.

Gus We will. I'm having a good time already. Hey, is that us the Sex Bomb's waving to? Well, I'll be blowed, she's waving at us!

Wally conceals his laughter by roughly drying his hair with his towel. Then he waves off L

Wally (*calling to the unseen "Sex Bomb"*) Coming! You go ahead and order, okay?

Black-out

SCENE 2

The hotel lawns. Afternoon

There are two beach loungers, a small table, a potted palm and a beach umbrella

When the Lights come up, Sylvie and Norma are preparing to sunbathe. Sylvie, Gus's wife, is in her mid-forties. She is all in pink. She slips off her jacket to reveal a frilly one-piece swimsuit. She wears pink sandals, a pink bangle, a pink hat and has a matching pink beachbag. During the scene, she sips from a drink served in a pineapple shell, over-decorated with fruit and flowers. Norma, already tanned, is wearing a brief, very chic bikini. She is about 28, and is very slim and sexy. She applies sun-cream from a small, expensive-looking jar. She also puts on some lipgloss

Sylvie This is the life. Now what could be better than this? Just tell me what could be better. Perfect weather, a lovely hotel, lovely food and people who speak your language! To my mind, this is paradise. Eh, Norma?

Norma (*languidly*) Mmmm. It does make a pleasant little break.

Sylvie A pleasant little break! By me this is our main holiday. Gus and I go away twice a year. Summer we come to a hotel like this. Easter we usually hire a caravan. But, between you and me, I'd rather be here and not have to shop. You get sick of catering, day in, day out.

Norma Yes. It is a drag having to cater all the time. Walt and I have a cook, but even so. Somebody has to tell her what to prepare and organize the shopping.

Sylvie is inclined to imitate Norma's movements. She produces a very large bottle of baby oil and applies it vigorously

Sylvie Have you got a Pick 'n Pay near you? We've got both. Pick 'n Pay *and* Checkers. But we get our veg from a little Indian. Are you near a shopping centre, where you live?

Norma I expect so. We're moving into our new place when we leave here. I told Walt I wasn't prepared to put up with the mess of renovations, so here we are. Not exactly Juan les Pins, but better than cement dust.

Sylvie checks to see if Norma is having her on

Sylvie Well. This place is good enough for me and Gus, I must say.

Norma Mmmmmmmm.

Sylvie Been married long?

Norma Couple of weeks.

Sylvie Couple of weeks! You dark horse—you didn't say a word. Your honeymoon! Well, imagine that. It takes me back to when we had ours. Nothing fancy like this—well, the hotel wasn't even here in those days. Gus and I stayed at a guest house over that way. (*She indicates*) We had a pair of li-los. In a pink they were. I've always been fond of pink. Anyway, every morning after breakfast, we'd come down to the beach and stake our claim for the day. Gus would blow up the li-los and lay them down, side by side. Gus is very neat, very orderly— picked it up in the army, I dare say. And then we'd lie there, making plans, working out our future. We got our money's worth out of those li-los, make no mistake. I used to say to

Gus, "The holiday hasn't begun till there's air in the li-los."
And then one year . . .

Norma (*wryly*) Gus ran out of breath?

Sylvie (*briskly*) Perished. All sticky and full of little holes. Ah,
what's the use in being sentimental. Gus and I have had twenty
years and never a day's regret. Hope you'll be able to say the
same, dear.

Norma Thank you.

Sylvie (*after a pause*) Planning on a family?

Norma No way. I'm not the maternal type and besides, Walter's
already got a family.

Sylvie Oh—you mean . . . Oh. I see. Well, if he's already got a
young family . . .

Norma Twin sons, aged twenty, and a daughter of eighteen.

Sylvie Oh. We've just got the two. A boy and a girl. Well.
Imagine that. On your honeymoon, eh? When Wally intro-
duced us all last night he never let on, the sly dog. But men
are like that. They often miss the drama in a thing.

Norma We've been living together for months, and this is
Walter's second marriage. I expect he doesn't think it's all that
dramatic any more. Otherwise he wouldn't be taking a nap,
would he?

Sylvie Gus is exactly the same, exactly. He worships his afternoon
nap. I told him the other day he's letting himself go, turning
into an old man. But they get like that when middle age arrives.
Eating and sleeping's all they want on holiday. (*She sits up,
glances around to make sure she won't be overheard*) Frankly,
the other thing is more or less dead as far as we're concerned.
I tried everything. Read advice columns, marriage guidance,
even phoned up Lifeline once, I was so desperate.

Norma sits up, interested for the first time

Norma I thought Lifeline dealt with suicides?

Sylvie That's right. Don't think I didn't give it a thought from
time to time. The truth is, dear, wonderful as he is in other
ways, Gus was never that interested. I used to think he was
being considerate, but once the children arrived . . . Of course,
I'm over it now, but at the time I thought it was my fault.

Norma And how old was Gus when he became asexual?

Sylvie Asexual?

Norma When he stopped making love to you?

Sylvie Early forties or so, he really ground to a halt. Ah well, as I say, I'm over it now. I lead a full life, keep myself busy. Did Wally's first wife pass away, or . . .? (*She pops a sweet into her mouth*)

Norma Alive and well and remarried, thank God. Most of the alimony fell away when she married again. Why didn't you take a lover?

Sylvie (*lying back*) I—I couldn't do a thing like that to Gus, dear. I mean, it's not his fault that desire died, is it? No, I kept myself busy and I'm over all that now.

Norma (*lying back*) Walt's sensational. in bed. That's what attracted me to him in the first place.

Sylvie (*shocked and thrilled*) In the first place indeed! I can see you're a bit of a card, my girl. But tell me all about when you met him. I love hearing how couples met.

Norma (*smiling*) He was a lonely business man and I was an out-of-work model . . .

Sylvie Go on.

Norma We fell in love. What else is there to tell?

Sylvie But it must have been very difficult. Him with big kids and everything . . .

Norma It wasn't so difficult once he made up his mind. And once she saw that Walt was determined, his ex came round. Then it was all over, bar the lawyers. (*She yawns*)

Sylvie (*after a long pause*) You know Norma, I feel close to you in a funny sort of way. It's as if I've known you a long time.

Norma Mmmmmm . . .

Sylvie Just now when you asked me why I didn't take a lover. I said I didn't because of Gus. You see Gus is a very special sort of person really. Very loyal for one thing—and generous. He wanted us to have everything, me and the children. One Christmas, about five years ago, he brought home a Portaswim brochure and told me to choose the one I wanted. We cleared a section of the garden—we lost our veggie patch, but it was worth it—and they came to give us an estimate. The foreman— well, the foreman was a lovely young chap. Very tanned and healthy looking. He was showing me the brochure and he said it would look even better if they had a photo of me in a bikini as part of the advert. I just laughed, as you can imagine. I was going on for forty and well past bikinis! But then, when the pool was installed, I thought to myself, why not? Now I've got my own private pool, why shouldn't I wear a bikini? (*She pauses, gazing at Norma's figure, and sighs*) A week later, I was sitting on the lawn, drying my hair, when he came back—said he'd come to check the filtration unit. (*She leans on her elbow and assumes a faraway expression*) He said he wished he had his camera and that he'd like a cup of tea and then he followed me into the kitchen and that was that. (*Her lips tremble, she rummages for a pink tissue in her beachbag*) I don't know what came over me. I just felt so young standing next to him. And he had a lovely smell, some sort of aftershave lotion I suppose. Afterwards, I just couldn't believe what I'd done. And I couldn't face the Portaswim. Even today, when I see Gus swimming with the kids, I feel terrible. Terrible. (*She blows her nose*) My goodness, Norma, you must be wondering why I'm telling you all this. I've never told a soul, not even my own sister. Yet somehow I feel I can trust you. I mean I somehow know you'd never say a word, never. You're that sort of person, aren't you, Norma?

Norma doesn't stir and Sylvie leans forward to look more closely

Norma?

Norma has dropped off to sleep. Sylvie stares at her, bewildered. After a few seconds, she begins to cry silently. If she sheds tears they should not be wiped away. She doesn't move at all

Slow fade to Black-out

SCENE 3

The beach, as SCENE 1. *Early morning*

Wally and Gus jog on stage. Gus is sunburned pink. They run on the spot, both looking very earnest. After a few seconds, Wally sneaks a look at his all-purpose watch. They jog on, then Wally's watch buzzes. The session is over. They slow down and stop, but during the scene they exercise various sections of their bodies

Wally That's the ticket! Never felt better in my life. How's your wind this morning?

Gus Coming along nicely. Trouble is, I don't do much at home. We've got a pool but the kids have lost interest lately and somehow the idea of swimming back and forth on my own doesn't appeal. Sylvie's got no interest in it either. You know how women are—couldn't wait to get a pool, then never as much as wets her big toe. Your Norma like exercise?

Wally Oh yes, yes. She's not particularly fond of swimming, but Norma's a great all-rounder. Horseriding, tennis, even fancies flying lessons once we've settled down. Keeps you on your toes having a live-wire like Norma around.

Gus (*after a pause*) Expensive business, flying. Was your first good lady a sporting type, Wal?

Wally Huh. You must be joking. If I'd kept to her pace I'd be in a wheelchair by now. Let herself go, Lily did. She was never what you'd call *petite*, but the last few years . . .! (*He pauses*) But I'm not saying she didn't have good qualities. On the contrary. Very well-liked as a matter of fact. Married again like a shot and I'll say this for her, she turned out more sophisticated over the divorce than I thought she would. We're quite good friends today. Makes life a lot easier, especially when there are kids to consider.

Gus Now that's something I can never understand. A couple liking each other enough to be friends, yet getting divorced after all those years of marriage. I can never make head nor tail of that.

Wally Depends on the people concerned. For me, friendship wasn't enough. I could feel old age coming on, creeping up on me. Spastic colon, backache, migraine, indigestion. All brought on by you know what? By *boredom*, that's what, *boredom*.

Gus Oh, I dunno about that. I mean we're all getting older aren't we? It's something we've got to face, like it or not. I'm not saying I don't understand you—I had my own crisis a few years back. You wouldn't credit what started it off—a bloody car of all things. A Jag. An XJ-six. I was parking my Cortina in the office parking bay one morning and I noticed it, parked in the visitors' section. I swear to God it was like a silver bullet. Beautiful lines, real leather upholstery, automatic windows—the works. Well, I just stood there like a lemon staring at it, thinking how I could sweat my guts out till the day I dropped and I still couldn't afford a car like that. Or the sort of house that goes with it. A kind of panic crept over me. You've had it, boy, I said to myself. There's no way you're gonna find yourself in the XJ-six bracket—and the sooner you face it the better!

Wally (*smiling*) You call that a crisis?

Gus The thing was, I couldn't talk myself out of it. I mean it wasn't the first time I'd realized I wasn't tycoon material. Sylvie and I would have a good laugh about things like that. I'd say to her, joking like, "Well love, barring a bit of luck on the jackpot, it doesn't look as if you'll get your mink." We'd have a good laugh, as I say. Sylvie would make me look around and count my blessings: "You've got your health, a comfortable home, a pool, a colour TV, a washing machine, a Hammond organ, two holidays a year," she'd say. "What more could a family want?" Well, usually it worked, thinking about the family and so on. But that morning, no amount of washing machines could put me right. I got back in the Cortina and sat there, wasting the firm's time.

Wally Ah well, comes a time in a man's life when . . . (*He tails off*)

Gus (*lost in his story*) Do you believe in fate, Wally?

Wally I believe people control their own destiny, get what they deserve. Call it fate if you like. Why?

Gus Because I opened a newspaper then, and the page I turned to was the Classified. Births, marriages, the personal column. And, there it was, I remember the actual wording to this day: "Isn't it time you pampered yourself a little? Let Valerie soothe away your cares. A qualified masseuse with golden hands is waiting to welcome you at Salon Imperial. Give us an hour of your time, and we'll take years off your age. Third floor, Hendrick House, over J.J.'s Motors, Victoria Street."

Wally (*laughing*) Hey, you dirty old bugger—had a bit on the side did you?

Gus It was the only time in my life I've been indiscreet. The first and last time and, by God, I've paid for it.

Wally Your Mrs find out, or what?

Gus Good God no—although I nearly broke down and told her a couple of times. Something terrible happened to me when I went into that place. I wasn't the type, you see. Horses for courses. Not everybody's the type when all's said and done.

They knew what they were about but none of their goings-on made the slightest difference.

Wally What the hell happened?

Gus Nothing, to put it bluntly. And the same ever since. I'm not saying I was the world's greatest lover, but that little lark laid me dormant for life. I wasn't the type, as I say, but the Jag., the XJ-six ... It was as if I couldn't stand the thought that I was where I was and the owner of that car was where he was. I kept thinking that going to a massage parlour would be an XJ-six sort of thing to do. Just for the once, I thought, live like the other half. Chuck away your respectability. Do something reckless. But it was a mistake, you see, going against the grain like that.

Wally So, big deal. What was so terrible? Know what I'd do if I were you? I'd either make up my mind to forget it, or tell your wife and get it over with. Make a joke of it—you said yourself nothing happened. How must she feel, living like a nun for years?

Gus It would kill her, Wally, kill her. Sylvie's always been modest, almost timid, in that respect. I wouldn't be surprised if she felt relief when things petered out. It's different for you, a man with your drive. You decided to start again and to hell with the consequences. A person has to be born with that kind of courage.

Wally You think it was easy. You think telling Lily and the kids was a piece of cake? She'd been a good wife to me. We'd been through a lot together and I must say she ran that house beautifully. Always a nice hot dinner waiting, preceded by a few tasty snacks to whet my appetite. The kids home all bursting to tell me their latest news. Lily used to make them speak in turn. "Give Dad a chance to get his breath," she'd say, "one at a time, one at a time." We never missed a dinner together. No matter how late I worked, Lily would be waiting, the food nice and fresh, a drink in my hand as I walked in. And then we'd talk about this and that. "What do you think, Wally," she asked me one night. "So-and-so had highlights done, would you like me to have highlights?" The kids and I laughed. I mean Lily was Lily, wasn't she? A wife and mother. What difference would highlights make?

Gus I can't say I agree with that. A woman needs a bit of attention, specially in middle age, Wal.

Wally I know, but that's the point. Lily had become too much of a wife and mother. She'd lost her mystery, her intrigue. There was no feeling of romance.

Gus (*after a pause*) I don't suppose she found you all that mysterious, after twenty-odd years.

Wally (*getting excited*) Then she could've done something about it. She could've gone out there and made a grab at life instead of sitting indoors, making me feel guilty! Look at me: I'm a young man, relatively speaking. The generation gap's not what it used to be. Today a man isn't over the hill just because he's got a couple of grey hairs, for Pete's sake! Vadim, Aznavour, Trudeau.

Gus looks blank

You won't catch them playing bowls—that's for bloody sure. You see, that's where Lily and I couldn't agree. By her the world is split into two: young people and old people. Let me give you an example. I needed a couple of suits, a few shirts and so on. And I decided to give this new boutique a try. I didn't feel like a misfit while I was in the shop—as a matter of fact, the proprietor congratulated me on my physique, said a lot of the gear could have been designed with me in mind. But when I showed the stuff to Lily, she hit the roof! Went off into the deep end!

Gus Gone overboard cost-wise, had you?

Wally (*impatiently*) Cost, schmost. She said I looked like an old actor trying to hide his age, wanted me to take the clothes back before the kids saw them. Said they'd be embarrassed to see their dad done up like a flyboy. (*He pauses*) Ahh, what's the use, Lily was always conservative. In her outlook, her choice of furniture, everything. I wish you could see what Norma's planning for our new place. Giant cushions instead of a suite, quadrophonic sound, a waterbed, a conversation pit. She's full of ideas—very creative, very original, very . . . laid back.

Gus Sounds like quite a change from the traditional, eh?

Wally That's for sure. Of course, Norma's caused a bit of a stir among my friends. You know how po-faced some of these middle-aged women can be—bitter with their lot and can't stand anybody else expressing a bit of individuality. But Norma can take care of herself—she doesn't turn a hair. In any case, we see more of her crowd these days. Once you get into their way of thinking, they're very stimulating. You'd be surprised. All I can say is, thank God I had the guts to make the move before it was too late. I've never felt better.

Gus Anyway, it's all water under the bridge now. Like it or not, what's done is done. It all came out in the wash and here we are on our hols, enjoying ourselves.

Wally I asked her once why she didn't kick up a stink. She told me she didn't want the kids upset. Said she saw me with Norma and gave up the ghost. I was upset over that. I thought she'd want to fight for me. But she said it wasn't her style. "You know how we feel about you, me and the children," she said, "the choice is yours." (*He becomes distressed*) I mean, you can see how she bloody well *pushed* me into it, can't you? Bloody fat bitch. She bloody well forced me to go through with it by not putting up an argument. My attorney was expecting an argument, Norma was, I was!

Gus (*concerned*) Take it easy, no point in getting yourself all het up. The way I see it she just wanted to keep her pride intact. I mean it was all she had left. You say she was overweight? No wonder she didn't want to compete with the likes of Norma— she would've been making a fool of herself, I can understand that all right.

Wally suddenly stabs at the rock with the sole of his foot, then turns his back, facing upstage, very tense. Gus looks out to sea, does a couple of armswings, glances at Wally. He approaches cautiously, and, after a couple of false starts, gently puts his hand on Wally's shoulder and administers a couple of pats

That's all in the past, as I say. Come on now, have you forgotten you're on honeymoon? The ladies will be wondering where we've got to. How about a quick dunk? I'll go in and test the water and if it's—what did you say the other day . . .?

Wally (*very flat*) Champagne.

Gus That's it. If it's champagne, I'll give you the nod, okay?

Wally nods silently

Gus, suddenly very cheerful, beats his chest, runs on the spot for a few seconds and then either runs off into the "sea" (through the audience) or off R

After a pause, Wally turns round. His face is bright and smiling, his body energetic and raring to go. He watches the sea as if awaiting a signal from Gus, then nods and briskly hitches up his swimming-trunks

Black-out

SCENE 4

The hotel lawns, as SCENE 2. *Afternoon*

Norma is lying down on her beach lounger, her eyes closed. Sylvie is sitting on the edge of hers, wearing another set of matching beachwear. Her face and arms are bright red

Sylvie I'm telling you Norma, it was like a miracle. Afterwards I just lay there thinking—wondering if I'd dreamt it! So what do you think? I mean just like that, out of the blue.

Norma Perhaps it was the sea air—or the salt water, something like that.

Sylvie Perhaps—but it's never worked like that before. Right after he went jogging with Wally it was. Within an hour. In fact, I'm wondering if it wasn't something Wally said. Some chance remark that sort of sparked Gus's imagination. Or maybe they had a heart-to-heart, like we did.

Norma Doubt it. Men don't have heart-to-hearts. They think it's macho to keep a stiff upper lip. (*She laughs*) Maybe your Gus gets switched on in five-year cycles—and yesterday was the day.

Sylvie Oh don't say that. I mean, I wouldn't like to think, you know, that I'd been reawakened all for nothing. I'll tell you though, he was amazing, like—like—a sultan!

Norma (*laughing*) My God, but your generation makes heavy weather of everything. Walt also came back from the beach rearing to go—not that it's so unusual in his case. But the way he carried on when I said I wasn't in the mood. You'd think it was the end of the world.

Sylvie I hope you didn't—refuse him, dear. It wouldn't seem right on honeymoon.

Norma Refuse him? You sound like something out of the Middle Ages. Close your eyes and think of England, is it? I'll bloody well refuse him whenever I damn well please. If that's the only reason he married me, he's got a surprise coming up!

Sylvie (*dreamily*) I have a feeling Gus and I are about to enter a wonderful new phase. The kids grown up. A bit more spare cash for luxuries like this. Oh, to think that only a couple of days ago I was worrying that the other business had come to an end. Tsk. Tsk. Well dear, just wanted to say hello for a bit. I'm off to pretty up for lunch. They're having two sheep on spits—and salads for Africa. What I really like about this place is that everything in the brochure is true. Of course, the rooms aren't quite as big as in the photos, but that's because the photographers stand on ladders, using wide-angle lenses. But the food is just as delicious as in the pictures and even the slogan they thought up is genuine.

Norma (*opening one eye*) What's the slogan?

Sylvie (*glancing around, then singing self-consciously*) "Come away, come away, dum-de-dum, something-dum, dum-de-dum—we'll make you feel brand new."

Both women laugh

Black-out

SCENE 5

The same as SCENE 1. *Early morning*

Wally and Gus are doing press-ups. They stop when Wally's watch buzzes and flop to the ground, exhausted, then get up and shake their arms etc.

Gus You know, Wally, I reckon it's a pity you and I don't live in the same town. We could jog of a morning, enjoy a chat now and then. I reckon we could've been friends—and the ladies seem to get on well.

Wally You jog in Jo'burg and I'll jog in Cape Town. Come Christmas and Rosh Hashama we'll exchange cards!

Gus I'm serious though, Wally. Our little chat did a lot for me the other day. I suddenly saw how safe I was, home and dry in a familiar harbour, so to speak. It put a different complexion on a number of things.

Wally (*after a pause*) One man's harbour is another man's prison. But I wish you luck, my friend. And calm seas, if that's what you want.

Gus We never got round to talking about our kids. You've got three, according to Sylvie. We've got the two, a boy and a girl. Suzanne's second-year nursing and Rodney's decided on electrical engineering. He's at tech. Lovely kids, if I say so myself.

Wally (*smiling*) My kids have been the best thing that ever happened to me. The boys are doing B. Comms. at U.C.T., my daughter's reading drama. She's a beauty, a real stunner. And all of them are bright as buttons, thank God.

Gus How did they take to the, ah, change-over?

Wally (*after a pause*) They love their old dad and they'd stand by me no matter what. Of course, it wasn't as if there was a custody battle or any of that sordid stuff. They carried on living with their mother because it suited all of us. But we couldn't be closer, couldn't be closer. A wonderful relationship.

Gus That's good news then. I mean, let's face it, I've heard of cases where the kids take sides . . .

Wally (*shaking his head vigorously*) No way. No way. Loyal right through. Linda wanted to come on this holiday, in fact. Thinks the world of me, my little Linda does. Of course, I'm not saying she doesn't love her mother, but you know how it is if you're lucky. Father and daughter. Lovely. I don't think she'd let anything come between us.

Gus (*probing*) And the boys?

Wally Sports. Studies. Girlfriends. I'm into everything they do. What can I say? They insist on involving me. Ask for advice non-stop. And, of course, I'm at their disposal. Dad this and Dad that. My secretary is worn out answering calls. But I want to tell you, Gus—I love every minute of it!

Gus And what about him—your ex-wife's new husband?

Wally What about him?

Gus *Vis-à-vis* the kids, I mean. Get on well, do they?

Wally Let me put it this way. He's Lily's husband, but he'll never be my kids' father.

Gus Ah well, time for a swim. The last one for me, eh?

Wally I'll miss you after today.

Gus I know you don't approve, but I'm going to dip in the pool being as it's my last day. I like a pool, as I say. Ours isn't anything lavish like the one at the hotel. In point of fact it's just a Portaswim. Model Two, a kidney shape. More for plunging than swimming.

Wally (*smiling*) You like a pool, I prefer the freedom of the sea. Each to his own, Gus.

Gus Before I go, there's something I'd like to say. I hope you won't take it amiss?

Wally (*getting his petrol bottle out from beneath the rock*) Fire away.

Gus It's in the nature of a confession, in a way. You see, when I saw you with . . .

Wally (*smiling*) Old S.B. the Sex Bomb!

Gus You were a good sport about that, I must admit. But anyway, when I saw you and Norma together—she was waiting at the hotel entrance and you drove up from the parking lot in your sports car, I said to myself, Gus, I said, there goes the man you'll never be. There goes the man you've been hankering to be all your life. He's got it all. Money. Beautiful young wife. Holidays every five minutes. The whole toot. It's wanting to be a man like you that landed me up queer street—over J.J.'s Motors to be exact. I'm going to put my cards on the table, Wally—I was up to here (*he indicates the level of his nose*) with envy. No, never mind *envy*—good old-fashioned jealousy.

Wally (*embarrassed*) Come on, Gus. There's no need . . .

Gus Let me finish. Please. We're equal here and I'd like to have my say. In the past few days I've come to terms with my life, compared my lot with yours. And the outcome is—and naturally there's no disrespect intended—I'd rather be me. Middle-aged wife, humdrum job, firm's Cortina, packaged holidays and all. At last, at long bloody last, I can honestly say I'm satisfied being Gus Armstrong.

Wally (*smiling*) Well, if I've helped you appreciate what you've got, I'm glad. What more can I say?

Gus You don't have to say anything, Wally. I've spoken my piece and I'll be on my way. Well met, as they say in the classics.

They shake hands and clap each other on the upper arm

Wally Say good-bye to Sylvie for me.

Gus Will do. Take care, and all the best. (*He picks up his towel and drapes it round his neck*)

Gus jogs off L. *Just before he exits, he waves jauntily, but without looking back*

Wally looks after him then sits on one of the rocks. A seagull cries plaintively. Wally's head swivels as he watches it circling overhead. Suddenly he jumps up, gropes for an imaginary stone and hurls it at the gull, which is now flying out to sea, its cries becoming distant. As he throws the stone with all his strength, Wally shouts at the gull

Wally (*angry and desperate*) SHUT UUUUUP! (*He lowers his arm and gazes around. His face is anguished. He scans the horizon. He makes a supreme effort to rearrange his features and begins to jog on the spot. His delivery becomes jovial and hearty*) Hup hup hup hup . . . got to keep fit. Then into the sea. It's champagne! A tonic! I've never felt better in my life! (*He jogs on, faster and faster, smiling*)

Slow fade to Black-out

CURTAIN

FURNITURE AND PROPERTY LIST

SCENE 1

On stage: 2 large rocks (polystyrene). *Beneath one:* plastic bag containing bottle of petrol and wad of cotton-wool (for **Wally**)
SWIMMING sign in umbrella holder
Small mound of sand
A few pebbles
Towel (for **Wally**)
Off stage: Towel (**Gus**)
Personal: **Wally**: wristwatch
Gus: comb in waistband of swimming-trunks

SCENE 2

On stage: 2 beach loungers
Beach umbrella in holder
Small table. *On it:* drink in pineapple shell, decorated with flowers, fruit and a straw (for **Sylvie**)
Potted palm
Beachbag. *In it:* small jar sun-cream, lipgloss (for **Norma**)
Beachbag. *In it:* large bottle of baby oil, tissues, bag of sweets (for **Sylvie**)

SCENE 3

On stage: As Scene 1

SCENE 4

On stage: As Scene 2

SCENE 5

On stage: As SCENE 1 plus towel for **Gus**

LIGHTING PLOT

Property fittings required: nil
2 exteriors: a beach and the hotel lawns

To open: effect of early morning light

Cue 1	When ready *Black-out*	(Page 1)
Cue 2	When ready *Return to opening lighting*	(Page 1)
Cue 3	**Wally:** ". . . and order, okay?" *Black-out*	(Page 5)
Cue 4	As SCENE 2 opens *Bring up sunny afternoon light*	(Page 5)
Cue 5	**Sylvie** cries silently *Slow fade to Black-out*	(Page 9)
Cue 6	As SCENE 3 opens *Bring up early morning light*	(Page 9)
Cue 7	**Wally** hitches up his swimming-trunks *Black-out*	(Page 15)
Cue 8	As SCENE 4 opens *Bring up sunny afternoon light*	(Page 15)
Cue 9	**Sylvie** and **Norma** laugh together *Black-out*	(Page 16)
Cue 10	As SCENE 5 opens *Bring up early morning light*	(Page 16)
Cue 11	**Wally** jogs on faster and faster, smiling *Slow fade to Black-out*	(Page 19)

EFFECTS PLOT

SCENE 1

No cues

SCENE 2

No cues

SCENE 3

Cue 1   **Wally** sneaks a look at his watch   (Page 9)
Pause, then buzz of watch alarm

SCENE 4

No cues

SCENE 5

Cue 2   When ready   (Page 16)
Buzz of watch alarm

Cue 3   **Wally** sits on rock   (Page 19)
Seagull's cries

Cue 4   **Wally** hurls imaginary stone at seagull   (Page 19)
Fade seagull's cries

MADE AND PRINTED IN GREAT BRITAIN BY
LATIMER TREND & COMPANY LTD PLYMOUTH
MADE IN ENGLAND

9 780573 121241